KEEPAHEAD PRESS
ARCHITECTURAL THEORY TEXTS

The series offers texts that are significant for an understanding of the history of architecture but that are presently out of print or not available in English translations.

- Heinrich Wölfflin, *Prolegomenon to a Psychology of Architecture* (1886). German text, and English translation by Michael Selzer. Paperback $12.50.
- August Thiersch, *Proportion in Architecture* (1883), and Heinrich Wölfflin, *A Theory of Proportion* (1889). English translations by Michael Selzer. Illustrated from the original versions. Paperback $12.50.
- Roland Freart, sieur de Chambray, *A Parallel of the Antient Architecture with the Modern in a Collection of Ten Principal Authors who have written upon the Five Orders...* Translated by John Evelyn (1664). Paperback $17.50.

Also by Michael Selzer from KeepAhead Books

- *The Symmetry Norm and the Asymmetric Universe*
- *Footnotes from a Bookseller's Life*
- *Renewing the Fear, A Jew goes to Berlin*
- *Snuffing up the Wind. Theomonarchism in the Biblical Text*

August Thiersch

Proportion in Architecture

&

Heinrich Wölfflin

A Theory of Proportion

Translations by Michael Selzer

KeepAhead Press Architectural Theory Texts No. 2

KeepAhead Books
Colorado Springs, 2017

For Robin Norris
賢い友人

ISBN-10: 1543211666
ISBN-13: 9781543211665

10 9 8 7 6 5 4 3 2

Table of Contents

TRANSLATOR'S NOTE

August Thiersch's, "Die Proportionen in der Architektur" was published in eds. Durm, Ende, Schmitt and Wagner, *Handbuch der Architektur unter Mitwirkung von Fachgenossen.* Part IV. Darmstadt: Diehl, 1883, pp. 38-77; and Heinrich Wölfflin's "Zur Lehre von den Proportionen", in *Deutsche Bauzeitung* (Berlin) v. XXIII, in 1889. Wölfflin's article appeared three years after his dissertation (vol. 1 in our Architectural Series Texts), in which he had expressed his conviction that Thiersch's "law" of proportion "is the same law that Nature follows in her creations".[1]

In translating technical terms used by Thiersch that seemed to me to be ambiguous or obscure, I have consulted an earlier translation, known to me only in typescript, by an American architect, Nathan Clifford Ricker (1823-1924). Ricker's translation is not without its problems, and evidently is based on a different version of Thiersch's text from the one used here.

Thiersch's primary objective in *Proportionen in der Architektur* is to identify the relationship of the parts of a structure to each other, and to the structure as a whole, that results in a beautiful building. He uses a number of terms for this result and it is unclear what if

---

[1] Heinrich W Wölfflin, *Prolegomenon to a Psychology of Architecture,* Colorado Sprins 2017, p. 31.

any difference in meaning he attached to them. I use "harmony" only in the relatively few instances when he uses "*das Harmonische*", and "concordance" for his "*Uebereinstimmung*". This and certain other synonymous terms may perhaps be understood as instrumental, referring, that is, to the methods that must be employed if the result, *das Harmonische*, is to be achieved.

It is probably through Wölfflin's brief note, translated in this volume, that Thiersch's "law" became well-known. In particular, Wittkower's highly influential views on the Renaissance theory of proportion are derived directly from these two sources.

Readers will want to determine for themselves how accurate the drawings are on which Thiersch and Wölfflin – not to mention Wittkower - based their conclusions.[2]

-    Michael Selzer

---

[2] See Michael Selzer, *The Symmetry Norm and the Asymmetric Universe,* Colorado Springs, 4rd. ed., 2017, Chapter 8.

August Thiersch
Proportion in Architecture

INTRODUCTION

There are in architecture laws that, when observed, ensure that a structure will be beautiful, and when ignored that it will be marred. To search out and formulate these laws is a task that science cannot ignore. We seek every principle that can be deduced directly from aesthetic feeling and can be grasped and justified by reason.

As far as proportions are concerned, it is very certain and applicable in all contexts that the parts of a structure must stand in a proper relationship to each other and to the whole. But the question is how this relationship is to be defined, whether it can be expressed in numbers or whether it can be referred back to simple geometric figures.

In music it is possible to use numbers to determine the relationship of notes that harmonize together (*zusammenstimmen*). Notes differ in the number of their vibrations. They harmonize when their vibrations coincide or dovetail with one another. Physicists have discovered a similarity to this in the effect that colors have on the eye. It would be mistake, however, for all that it is one on which many theories have already foundered, to infer from this that the eye prefers certain simple ratios in the dimensions of forms and figures. If, for example, one of two notes that sound well together is lowered or raised slightly, complex or irregular vibrations occur in the eardrum, creating a discordant sound (*Miston*). But on the other hand, when a right-angled figure whose sides are in a 2:3 ratio has its length altered slightly, the eye remains completely unaware of it. However, simple numerical relationships play a role in the dimensions of ancient structures, as detailed investigations have shown.

Viollet-le-Duc believed that ancient builders used as their models three different triangles: the Egyptian triangle of the pyramids, the right-angled isosceles, and the equilateral. But the way in which these figures are incorporated on the Arch of Titus in Rome or in the cross-section of the cathedral of Amiens is less than persuasive.[3]

One can say, all in all, that these elements do not reach very far. If they embodied the laws of beauty we would have to say, regretfully, that architecture would be condemned to monotony. The massive and the powerful are as valid as the slender and the graceful. In organic

---

[3] See Henszlmann, E: *Théorie des Proportions appliquèes dans l'architecture depuis la douzièeme dynastie des rois ègyptiens jusq'au XVIe siècle.* Part 3, Egyptian style. Doric Order. Paris, 1860.

Aures, A: *Nouvelle thèorie du module, déduite du text meme de Vitruve et application de cette theorie à quelques monuments de l'antiquité grecque et romaine.* Nimes, 1862.

Viollet-le-Duc: *Entretiens sur l'architecture.* Vol.1. Paris 1863. (9th observation, p.395ff.)

Viollet-le-Duc: *Dictionnaire raisonnè de l'archiecture francaise*, etc. Vol7. Paris 1864 (p.532, article on "Proportion").

Nature they all have their different characters, as for instance with trees, each with its distinctive beauty. By the same token, it is possible that the range of possible architectural styles has not yet been exhausted.

We look, accordingly, for a law that accommodates a great diversity of architectural styles and re-mains valid even in the most varied circumstances.

The Similarity of Figures

One step toward the discovery of such a law was taken when the German thinker Zeising[4] pointed to the Golden Section, the fixed proportion that Euclid taught, by which the smaller portion of a straight line is in the same ratio to the larger, as that has to the whole. We bid it welcome and go yet another step further.

It is the fixed *proportion altogether*, and the *similarity of the figures,* that Euclid addresses in the Sixth Book of his *Elements.* We find by studying the most successful works of all time that in every structure a basic form repeats itself: that the individual parts constitute similar figures in their arrangement and form. There are countless numbers of different figures that, in and of

---

[4] Ziesing, A: *Neue Lehre von den Proportionen des menschlichen Körpers*. Leipzig, 1854.

themselves, cannot be called either beautiful or ugly: harmony (*das Harmonische*) arises from the repetition of the main figure (*Hauptfigur*) of a work in its subdivisions.

This intimate relationship of the individual parts to the whole is especially observed in the works of Classical architecture, and accounts for their unified and harmonious appearance.

CHAPTER ONE: PROPORTION IN DORIC ARCHITECTURE.
Doric Temples

If that is the case it must be most apparent in Doric temples, whose proportions remained unchanged for centuries.

In fact, such concordance (*Ueber-einstimmung*) of all parts was nowhere achieved more completely than in the columnar construction of the Grecian Doric temple.

This is not to say that a definite, unalterable ratio was established. On the contrary, we can see, from the oldest known massive monuments in Selinus to the elegant marble temples of Attica, variations in the relationship between the overall structure and its components that at first glance appear to undermine its order. The relationship of a temple's length to its width, of the thickness of a column to its height, of the entablature's height to the height of the column, always vary: and yet, with few exceptions, almost every structure retains the concordance of its parts and presents an appearance that is harmonious in itself.

Two distinctive qualities present themselves to us. First, for specific parts of the structure, very simple numerical ratios that disappear from the later, artistic, temple architecture and make way for more complex ratios. Two, the geometric similarity of all analogous parts, which is strongly emphasized as a leading idea until Later Antiquity.

Numerical Ratios

The following simple numerical ratios are observed in ancient temples:

(1) The width and height of the cella, as well as of the pronaos, are identical;

(2) The breadth and height of the part of the cella façade that is visible from outside are in a ratio of 2 : 3 (figs. 1 and 2);

(3) The height of the columns is twice that of the distance between their axes ($h=2a$);

(4) The height of the architrave equals one-third of the distance between the columnar axes, or the length of the blocks.

The first condition is met when the height of the pronaos to the top of the ceiling beams is the same as the distance between the walls, or by that token, that the distance of opposite antae is equal to the height of the pronaos up to the top edge of the architrave (*figs.* 2 and 5). It follows from the third and fourth conditions that as a rule the architrave and the frieze are the same height, and that the height of the entablature without the geison is three times that of the pillars. The primitive temple at Selinus meets these conditions only in part.[5] By contrast, the ratios mentioned above are complied with in the following temples: Temple A in Selinus; the temple of Poseidon in Paestum; the temple of Zeus in Olympia; and the temple of Athena in Aegina.

These numerical rations recommend themselves in part on practical grounds; they facilitated the design and execution of plans; and perhaps were also prescribed by cultic ordinances. But they were no more valid for all applications and all periods than any other canonical ratios.

But as architecture took on a bolder attitude and freed itself from the old priestly bonds, men began to abandon the restrictions on the height of columns, making them taller, so

---

[5] The oldest ratio of columnar height according to Pliny (*Hist. Nat.* I. 36, c.23) was one-third of the temple.

that the column without the abacus, or its shaft alone, reached the height of $h=2a$. The architrave block retained for a longer time the ratio of 1:3. As a result, the entablature remained lower in relationship to the column.

However, the other law remained in effect: that the parts of a building are to be analogous to each other and to the whole. The concordance (*Uebereinstimmng*) consists in the first instance of the similar configuration of the two main parts, the shell and the kernel – that is to say, the peristyle and the cella; and in the second instance, of the repetition of the same form and proportions in the parts of the entablature.

The Ground Plan

(1) A comparison of the ground plan, for all the variations of length and breadth, nevertheless reveals the intention to give the outer line of the peristyle (the edge of the upper step) the same form as the interior of the cella (*figs.* 3 and 16). The porticos in front of the cella and behind it are very deep, those along its sides are shallow, an arrangement that that cannot be accounted for on structural or practical grounds. If one draws the diagonal of the rectangle of the uppermost step, it either coincides with the diagonal of the interior of the cella or runs parallel to it. With the exception of the Theseus temple in Athens this holds true for the plans of

all Doric temples, even for the small, ancient temple cella on the acropolis of Selinus.

Cella and Temple Facades

(2) The cella façade, to the extent that it is visible from the outside, down to the bottom of the inner architrave, and the façade of the entire temple including its stylobate, form two similar rectangles (in the archaic style a ratio of 2:3); the kernel and its shell are analogous (*Fig.* 4). One notices that, in order to achieve this concordance (*Uebereinstimmung*), it is necessary for temples with a broad span between the row of columns and the cella to have high entab-latures and stylobates, and that in temples with a narrower span lower entablatures are called for (*Figs.* 6, 7 and 8). It is for this reason too that sometimes, as in Paestum, the outer entablatures are lower and sometimes higher (Bassae) than the inner ones. In other words: *the colonnade increases the cella's relative height no less than its breadth.*

ENTABLATURE

(3) The two triglyphs enclosing a metope, along with the portion of the cornice above them, make up an enclosure that, when one is looking at it from the front, shows itself in many ways to be analogous to the entire structure. As the cella walls and the columns enclose a half-

dark anteroom (the pronaos), so does the ensemble of the frieze with the metopes. These seem like small spaces, open in the front and sheltering under the deeply-projecting roof; and like the pronaos of the cella, they are filled with sculptures. Closer inspection shows that both systems coincide in their proportions.

The figure of the metope varies from a square in the same way as the opening of the pronaos (*figs.* 9 and 10). The ratio of the triglyph's width to that of the metope is the same as the width of the portico (columns and walls together) to that of the pronaos (as measured between the antae). They are mostly simple numerical ratios:

Temple C, Selinus, 1:1

" of Poseidon, Paestum, 3:4

" of Concordia, Agrigentum, 2:3

" of Athena, Egina, 3:5

" of Apollo, Bassae, 3:5

Narrow cellas therefore call for narrow metopes, and wide porticos for wide triglyphs.

Moreover, the band at the top of the metope is analogous to the inner architrave, while the projecting mutules correspond to the porch. A comparison shows that in fact the mutule system has the same ratio to the metope as the entablature to the cella.

These parts of the entablature and the architrave fillet with its regula were always identified by their coloring as belonging together.

Further, the geison is to the triglyph frieze (along with the mutules) as the entire entablature is to the cella walls and columns. In fact, the ratio of the height of the geison to the height of the frieze is almost always the same as the height of the entablature is to the height of the columns (reckoned with the ratio of the mutule system to the frieze): compare the corresponding profiles of the temples of Paestum and Aegina and the Parthenon (*figs*. 11, 12 & 13). Thus the principle ratios of stylobate to column to entablature are repeated in the larger and smaller subsections of the entablature.

But a relation between the small and large sections is brought in the projections, especially with regard to the silhouette.

The entablature, to the extent that it projects sideways over the body of the cella, and the geison, the drip-molding and even the abacus of the capital (when viewed diagonally) form in projection figures similar to one another (comp. *figs*. 11 and 12). Usually, the extended diagonals of the front of the façade intersect the corners of these figures, and so fix the ratios of their breadth and height.

Façade of the Entablature

4) The following concordances between horizontal figures occur on the facade of the entablature.

The two pieces of the architrave placed above a column comprise a form that is, in accordance with archaic rules, 6 times as long as it is high (*fig.* 14). The same rectangle always shows this beam as a support for the abacus of the capital; this same figure is also formed by the entire entablature of the façade, and appears again in the delicate regula drops, which themselves appear as a small representation of the entablature of the facade, with its six conical supports.

The figure of the geison block, if its height be half that of the architrave, as is usually the case, is the same as that of the triglyph capital (1:6).

The Parthenon

And thus the façade of the Doric temple achieves a concordance that is realized even in its smallest detail and that is closely bound up with the number of its columns.

Only an architect of genius, like Iktinos, could allow himself to break with the traditional arrangement by giving the façade of the

Parthenon eight columns. With that, he gave up the concordance of the cella and metope, of the architrave block, of the entire entablature and of the regula. In doing so however he achieved a perfect conformity between the temple's interior and exterior such as had never been achieved in hexastyle structures.

Note how, in the plan (of the Parthenon), the interior space of the cella enclosed by columns conforms to the entire space enclosed by walls, and how this is again similar to the exterior outline of the cella and finally to the outer colonnade (*fig.* 15). Through this device it became possible to achieve in all sides a concordance between the cella and the (exterior) colonnade (*fig.* 16).

This happens both with and without the stylobate; in the latter case, if one calculates the architrave of the inner row of columns along with the height of the cella. The cella façade and that of the temple itself form a rectangle of 1:2 instead of 2:3.

Other relations noted are: the height and projection of the cornice as well as the height and projection of the entire entablature (over the walls on the cella's length) to the height of the columns (*fig.* 12). This figure delineates the protrusion of the drip-molding and the capital's abacus seen along the diagonal. On the capital of the Propyleum, which is very similar to that of the Parthenon, the geison projects further out to match the considerable depth of the portico.

Later Buildings

We see that in designing the Temple of Apollo in Bassae the builder of the Parthenon followed the hexastyle schema, but with a diminished expression of sturdiness than had previously marked Attic construction. The character of the building is determined by the form and proportions of the columns. This is the only living, so to speak fleshly, element in the rigid framework of the structure. The breadth and diminution of the shaft, the profile and projection of the echinus, differ in each temple, expressing the architect's taste and the prevailing notions of his time. In the archaic temple the strongly diminishing shaft and the fleshly widely-overhanging echinus convey a high degree of energy, which the columns use to brace themselves against the entablature. Later, as the columns became taller and the entablature relatively lower and lighter, men were satisfied with the suggestion of a modest display of power with capitals that were low and skinny in shape. The frame of the structure remained almost exactly the same; but meagerness and weakness replaced muscular power and energy.

Similarly, a close relationship between the column's diameter and certain dimensions of the structure. The triglyph's width was always either half of the lower or half of the middle diameter of the column. Because two triglyphs meet over one intercolumniation, the width of the triglyph must be in proportion to that of the metope, as the diameter of the column is to that of their intercolumniations (*Zwischenweiten*). *The compact placement of the columns, or their tightness, is mirrored again in the placement of the triglyphs.*

Further, it follows from what was said in 3, above about the relationship between the width of the triglyph and that of the pteron that in older buildings these too depended on the diameter of columns:

Temple/Location	Columnar diameter: intercolumniation	Triglyph: metope	Widths pteron:pronaos
Poseidon/Paestum	m* 3:4	3:4	3:4
Heracles/Akragas	m 3:4	3:4	3:4
Athena/Aegina	b* 3:5	3:5	3:5
Athena/Syracuse	m 2:3	2:3	2:3
Theseus/Athens	b 2:3	2:3	2:3
Parthenon/Athens	m 2:3	2:3	2:3
Apollo/Bassae	m 3:5	3:5	3:5

m = columnar diameter at middle; b = diameter at bottom

Proportions in Egyptian Architecture

It was, then, the analogy of forms that was regarded as good design in the construction of

Doric temples. It is inconceivable that this rule
was upheld unconsciously, merely on the basis
of instinct and mindless repetition. It appears
rather to have been passed on as a guild secret in
the workshops and construction sites of the
Greeks. Its first appearance is lost in the dark-
ness of prehistory.

We have reason to suppose that, just as there
was a canon for Greek sculptors, there was also
one much earlier for architectures, namely in
Egypt during the glorious 18th Dynasty.

We will not cause any annoyance by taking a
look back at the land of the pharaohs. The
Hellenic purists, who regard Greek art as a
product entirely home-grown in Greece, and
dismiss every suggestion of oriental or Egyptian
influence, are disappearing. The horizon of art
history has expanded. The works of Friedrich
Thiersch,[6] Roth,[7] and Julius Braun,[8] have not
been in vain. In what follows, we may take as
proven and accepted the connection of the
Doric style to Egyptian architecture.[9]

To be sure, the style of those huge structures
in Thebes, with their courtyards and pylons,

---

[6] On the epochs of fine art among the Greeks, 2nd. ed. Munich,
1829.

[7] *Geschichte underer abendlandischen Philosophie.* Vol. 2 *Geschichte der
griechischen Philosophie.* Mannheim 1858 (Pythagoras, p.260ff.)

[8] *Geschichte der Kunst,* Wiesbaden 1856-58. 2nd. Reber ed., 1873.

[9] Comp. also Part II, Vol.1 of this "Manual" (The Architecture of
the Greeks" by J. Durm, p.1)

evolved further in another direction, with the cella surrounded by a system of chambers; but a number of monuments from the beginning of that grand epoch display the simple plan, later abandoned or set aside, of a peripteral temple. The most precisely researched temple of this type, built by Amenophis III on the island of Elaphantine, is to a remarkable degree the prototype of the Doric temple (*fig.* 17).

In plan and elevation the cella is similar to the peristyle that encloses it; its façade, to the extent that it can be seen, likewise forms a rectangle with a ratio of 2:3; its base corresponds to the sub-structure of the whole.

In structures of the same period one notices, moreover, the same strictly-observed ratio of the architrave height to its length (1:3), evidently a rule worked out earlier in stone construction. The use of the diagonal of a rectangular figure for determining the width and height of an enclosure also seems to have been widespread. The cavetto cornices of doors and niches are always arranged accordingly.

Finally, the predominant plan of temples in Egypt, with its many enclosures, shows us, sometimes more and sometimes less clearly, the principle of the repetition the basic figure. This is given here by the cella in conjunction with the hall across from it. This arrangement is clearest in the temple architecture of the Ptolemies.

We are therefore not going too far when we say that, as Pythagorus of Samos brought mathematics to Egyptian scholars, so in the distant past architects, whose names are now lost, transplanted a type of temple architecture and the principle of analogy from the land of the Nile to the coast of Greece.

CHAPTER TWO: PROPORTION IN IONIC ARCHITECTURE.
The Ionic Temple in Attica

We return from this detour back to Greek architecture, fastening our gaze first on the Ionic temples of Attica and then of Asia Minor; and then reviewing the work of Roman architects.

The temple of Nike in Athens and the one on Ilissus, now vanished, have colonnades only in front of and behind the cella; the portico and cella coincide when seen from the front. As in the cella of the Doric temple, the height and breadth were required to be equal, while the ratio of length to width is different. The side view shows the same conformity of cella and colonnade that appears on the façade of Doric temples. To make the inner and outer figure the same, it was necessary for the short cella of the Nike temple (*figs.* 18 and 19) to have a tall entablature and a tall stylobate. On the temple of Ilissus these parts are required, because of the cella's oblong form, to be lower (*fig.* 23). Both rectangles have a ratio of 1:2.

The Erechtheion, a noteworthy example of an asymmetric but nevertheless harmonically arranged ensemble, obeys the law of conformity in another fashion.

Both the porticos attached to the sides of the main structure have the same plan (*fig.* 24) as it (2:3). With regard to dimensions, level and design they are altogether different, but in outline (the relation of breadth to height) they are similar to one another if one reckons the parapet on which the caryatids stand along with the height of the supports.

The composition of the entablature of this Ionic Attic temple is quite similar to that of the Doric entablature. Architrave and frieze are the same height as each other, though otherwise they are as different as they could possibly be. The architrave is plain or composed of horizontal layers; the frieze with its sculptured reliefs consists of a row of standing figures.

Above it is placed the cornice, just as the entire entablature over the columns, and the relation of the geison's height to that of the frieze is the same as the entablature's height to that of the columns. The heavy 1:3.5 ratio is repeated on the Nike temple (*fig.* 22), and the lighter 1:4.3 on the Erechtheion (*fig.*23). The overhang of the geison is in proportion to the projection of the entablature ove the cella façade.

The cornice, taken in a broader sense to include cymatium and the roof's slab, is again in the same relation to the entablature as it is to the height of the columns.

The same ratios on a larger scale return again in the structure of the caryatid portico; the statues are in the same ratio to their substructure and their entablature, as the sculptured frieze is in relation to the architrave and to the cornice.

Diverging from them, the Ionic entablature of Asia Minor consists of four courses that diminish progressively as they ascend. The temple at Priene (*fig.* 25) shows this, as do the temple at Magnesia and the Mausoleum of Halicarnassus.

As the architrave is to the frieze, so is the latter to the dentils and they to the cornice.

Each component of the series stands in the same proportion to the one that follows it, and the ratio of a section of the entablature to the sum of the layers that lie above it is always the same. *Fig.* 25 shows at attempt to construct a scale for the regular diminution of the sections. It will be observed that the height of the frieze is in reality greater than shown in this diagram, and one should keep in mind that the architrave molding always covers a portion of the frieze so that the frieze seems lower than it really is. Finally, it should is worth noting that cymation, or the crowning portion of a section of the entablature stands in a specific ratio to it. This holds for the Ionic entablature found in Olympia.

The same progressive diminution of the stone layers and their cymations is evident in the interior of the entablature where it abuts the coffers.

As for the plans of the temples in Asia Minor, they either follow the concordance of cella and peristyle of the peripteral Doric temple (Priene) or else take a second complete row of columns, resulting in a dipteral temple (Ephesus, Miletus).

By abandoning the inner row of columns, Hermogenes invented the pseudipteral temple. Because it was now possible to see more clearly through the portico than was the case in the dipteral temple, it became necessary to have the cella and peristyle conform to one another. Conformity was easier to achieve in the plan than in the elevation, where it was made possible only by separating a part of the body of the cella with a stringcourse (*Gurtgesim*), or by isolating the cella's substructure or sockel, as we see from the admittedly later templs of Aizanoi (fig.26), Aphrodisias and Baalbeck. The temple of Artemis in Ephesus also seems to have had a high sockel that, with respect to the columns, was decorated with sculptures.

Secular Greek Buildings

The few remains of Greek secular buildings also show us the same law of concordance. The front elevation of the Tower of the Winds in Athens the interior and exterior outline of the porticoes are similar to one another (*fig.*27). The two right angles are arranged concentrically, and the overall shape of the tower is arranged around the same center. As the entablature is to the columns, the cornice of the tower with the figural frieze is to it [the tower].

As in the Ionic of Asia Minor, the entablatures of the porticos consist of progressively diminishing layers (*fig.* 28); but when viewed diagonally their outline resembles the Corinthian capitals beneath them. It is the angle of the entablature that actually is most noticeable; they are on the same plane as the diagonal profile of the capitals. Both these profiles conform to one another in all essential points.

As the abacus of the capital is to the cup, so is the cornice to the entablature. The projection and height of these elements bear the same relationship in both these parts to the height of the overlapped bodies. The outline of the acanthus leaves corresponds to the projecting elements of the architrave.

The monument of Lysicrates shows the same correspondence of the profiles of the capitals and entablature, though, because of its circular shape it is not the diagonal but the normal profile that is expressed in the profile (*fig.* 29). The same is also evident in the Doric. In the monument of Trasyllus (*fig.* 30) in Athens, as in the temple of Artemis in Propylaia in Eleusis, the profiles of the capitals of the antae correspond in the main with those of the entablature. The projection of the abacus is the same as that of the geison; the molding of the antae's capital, with its fillets, is in proportion to the height of the entablature frieze and the smooth stripes of the architrave. The palmetto strip on the necking of Ionic antae and the wall of the cella is analogous to the figural frieze of the entablature.

CHAPTER THREE: PROPORTION IN ROMAN ARCHITECTURE

New forms emerge in Roman architecture; but despite all changes, the old basic ideas still persist.

The Italian temple has a portico only in front of the cella and stands on a tall substructure that can be climbed only up the front. Nevertheless, the same concordance is achieved here as in the Attic Ionic temples. Viewed from the side, the cella and the structure overall form similar figures (*fig.* 31). Here too most rectangles have simple numerical ratios, that are repeated. The substructure and the entablature add as much to the height of the cella, proportionately, as the projecting portico contributes to its length.

The flanks have the following ratios:

Temple of Fortuna Virilis, Rome 2:3

Temple of Jupiter, Pompeii 1:2

Temple of Antoninus and Faustina, Rome 1:2

The concordance is more complete in circular temples than in any other type. The visible cylinder of the cella is in conformity with the entire structure (the Temple of Vesta in Tivoli). If the columns stand on steps, only, the cella, in order not to appear too high, have a string course (Temple of Vesta in Rome).

We encounter the similarity of interior and exterior form in the manifold ground plans of temples of the imperial period. Where the cella is enclosed on both sides by porticoes, the facades of the cella and of the overall structure conform to one another (Temple of Mars Ultor and Temple of the Dioscuri in Rome). A string course on the cella separates it from the sockel, which makes it an analog to the columnar substructure. The similarity of cella and portico is carried the furthest in the Temple of Jupiter in Baalbek (*fig.* 32).

Even in very unconventional temple plans, like that of Concordia in Rome (*fig.* 33), where the portico in front of the cella is narrower than it, both nevertheless have similar forms. The portico of the Pantheon harmonizes with the circular structure in that both have the same ratio of width to height, for all that they are in other respects very different from one another. The pediment, though in and of itself far too high, is consistent with the dome that surmounts the cylinder.

The interior of the Pantheon, in its almost Greek purity, shows throughout examples of beautiful concordance. The similarity of height and breadth in the interior is repeated in the openings of the large niches. Finally, the columnar frames of the small altars harmonize with the pair of great pilasters that flank the mass of the pier and form a concentric, balanced, frame (*fig.* 34).

Triumphal Arches

Their original and harmonious design entitle the triumphal arches to special attention. The rule is consistently observed that pairs of columns or pilasters which serve as enclosures for the archway must be shaped like the archway itself. The interior pair of supports is surmounted by an arch and the exterior pair with a horizontal entablature, and this discrepancy is resolved by them having the same ratio of breadth to height.

In the gate of the river at Chamas (*fig.* 35) a rectangle, flanked by a pair of pilasters, repeats the shape of the overall structure. In the triumphal arch of Titus (*fig.*38) the square is seemingly used throughout as the basic figure, except that the attic is a little too tall, a flaw that is avoided in the arch of Titus at Beneventum.

In the triumphal arch of Trajan in Ancona (*fig.* 37) a ratio of 1:2 is employed for the vertical rectangle of the gateway, for the interior and exterior lines of the space containing the engaged columns, and also for the entire shape. The arrangement of the portal columns, furthermore, is enclosed by the mass of the structure with its same ratio of breadth to height. On the gate of Hadrian in Athens (*fig.* 39) three groupings of supports equidistant from one another enclose the thoroughfare, and the upper storey repeats the same shape.

The triumphal arches of Septimius Severus (*fig.* 40) and of Constantine (fig.41), each with its three openings, show the same concordance between the gate openings and their enclosures. For practical reasons, the openings on the side, which were for pedestrians, are narrower than the principal gateway which was intended for vehicles and horses. One must take here the broken sections of the entablature with the columns in order to compare them with the piers of the archway (*fig.*42). The inpost caps are analogous, by the clustering together of their parts, with the cornice. But if one takes alone the two columns that flank the main archway, they define a square central field (the height of the columns equaling the intercolumniation), which the mass of the entire structure encloses at the sides and on top by an equal width. Further, if one imagines the gateway filled with a crowd of people (approximately 2 meters tall), it too becomes square and conforms with the frame of columns. The side gateways then come closer to the shape of the main gateway.

The height of the attic of the Arch of Constantine, moreover, is designed in such a way that the middle archway is relatively speaking as tall as the side archways (*fig.* 42).

In other words: the façade is composed of three analogously shaped parts standing next to each other. As the horizontal entablature and the field for the inscription are above the main archway, so are the zones of reliefs and sculptures above the flanking gateways. Conformity in the proportions of the mass and variety in the treatment of the parts that are analogous to each other is the foremost principle of Roman design. Moreover, simple numerical ratios also play a role. The distances between the columnar axes are 2 : 3 : 2. The main gateway forms a rectangle of 3 : 4; the height of the pedestals is one-half that of the columns, etc.

Finally, the conformity between the parts of the structure that are laid on top of each other must be demonstrated. This is clearest in the side view of the triumphal arch (*fig.* 43). The division of the main storey into pedestal, column and entablature is repeated in the attic.

The ratio of these parts of the structure to each other is 2 : 4 : 1.

The pedestals of the columns as well as those of the statues are divided in entirely the same manner.

The repetition of the composition of the overall structure in the parts of its substructure is shown very clearly in the profile of the temple of Fortuna Virilis (*fig.* 44). The cornice of the substructure repeats that of the entablature, and the sockel of the substructure mirrors that of the substructure itself; the profile of the sockel conforms to the feet of the columns without the steps. The analogy between the parts of the pedestal and those of the entire order can be seen most exactly in the arch of Septimus Severus. The aedicule of the Pantheon should also be compared with the minute subdivisions of their bases.

Components of the Entablature

The repetition of the form of the large in the small is also evident in the components of the entablature. Although in Greek architecture the entablature is built up in an arrangement that reflects that of the ceiling and the roof, the parts of the Roman entablature is an entirely external decoration. The cornice with its embellishments constitutes the main part of the entablature and dominates the other parts.

The portions that crown the architrave are smaller and simplified versions, of if one will, forerunners of the cornice.

This type of concordance was already apparent in the profile of Greek entablatures; it is also very apparent in the profiles of Italian entablatures and dominates the components of the marble entablatures of imperial Rome. In the Greek entablatures the upper face of the architrave, with its moldings (*Wellen*) and its shielding plates (*deckenden Plättchen*) is a model of the entire (entablature) – comp. the Erechtheion, the temple of Nike, Priene, and the Tower of the Winds, *figs.* 23, 25, and 28. The divisions of the Italian entablature (*fig.* 45) is of a kind that the upper face of the architrave is to the parts that surmount it as the frieze is to the cornice (the caps over the doors of Cori, Tivoli and the entablatures at Pompeii).

Both kinds of arrangements are found in Roman profiles. The Greek principle is followed in the entablature of Nero (*fig.* 49) whose architraves have bipartite fascias and of the temple of Antoninus and Faustina (*fig.* 46), and also in the architraves with three divisions in the temples of the Dioscuri and of Concordia in the Forum Romanum. We find the Italian conformity in almost every other known example. As the cornice if to the frieze, so is the crowning of the architrave to the upper fascia (*fig.* 47). As a rule, the three main sections of the

entablature – the cornice, frieze and architrave –
are of the same height (excluding the cornice
cyma); and the crown molding of the architrave,
the upper fascia and the middle fascia with its
moldings, also form equal parts. The same
contrasting placement next to one another of
striated surfaces of the same height is repeated in
the lower section of the cornice.

Moreover, the cornice usually has the same
proportion to its lower portion as the fillet of the
architrave has to its molding (the orders of the
Colosseum, the Portico of Octavia, the aedicula
of the Pantheon, and the Dioscuri and Concordia temples). Where the crown molding of
the architrave has a cavetto in the manner of
Ionic Asia Minor (*fig.* 49 and the temple at
Palmyra, *fig.* 48, the cyma must always be taken
in comparison the projecting cornice. This also
happened in the Pantheon, in the temple of
Vespasian and in Trajan's forum.

Where recesses of the architrave are
decorated with leaves they exhibit a regular
increase in height. An example of this, and also
of the repetition of the main divisions of the
entablature in the subdivisions of the architrave,
is the beautiful cornice on the interior of the
Pantheon over the entrance (*fig.* 50).

A more important relation is that between
the profile of the column capital and that of the
entablature. As was shown earlier with regard to
the Tower of the Winds in Athens (see *fig.* 28),

both the profiles match each other when seen from the corner, as they also do in height. The geison, with or without the cyma, matches the abacus, and the three layers of the entablature the three rows of leaves of the bell. The modillons supporting the geison are analogs of the volutes, which nestle up against the abacus (*fig.* 51). When considered from this perspective, the Composite capital is entirely justified. The upper subdivisions of the cornice is anticipated by the strong and rich division of the cornice.

The same relationship can also be found in the plainer organization of the Roman Doric and the Tuscan orders, between profiles of the capitals of columns or pilasters and the entablature (*fig.* 52). Compare this to the Greek example (*fig.* 30).

While the Greek style places large, simple forms apparently directly opposite each other, but holds them in stronger dependence on the whole structure, Roman architecture, having loosened this connection, prefers to divide the entablature into parts that resemble itself. The elegance that this achieves compensates for loss of the the fine details of the Greek entablature. (Comp. the profiles of the substructure of Mars Ultor in *fig.* 53 and the theater of Marcellus in *fig.* 54.)

Statements of Vitruvius

Greek and Roman architects were guided by this basic principle, which leads to the question of whether it has been stated anywhere. Such an important theoretical point could neither be kept secret nor be treated as self-evident. We must look around and see whether this principle has not been committed to words in the writings of the Ancients.

Admittedly, the writings and commentaries of Greek and Roman architects about their temples are lost to us; but the work of the Roman architect Vitruvius, dedicated to Octavian, has been preserved, and because it is derived from Greek sources, we may hope for some information from it about our problem.

In fact he spoke about it in three places, even if not with the detail and precision that one might want to expect, yet clearly enough to allow us to understand that similarity of form was one of the transmitted laws of architecture.

First, where Vitruvius speaks in general of the laws of architecture (I. chap. 2), and then where he speaks of the constructions of temples in particular (II c. 1) he demands that "symmetry" be observed. He does not understand this to mean the equality of the two halves, in the sense of one side being the mirror image of the other – no special provision is needed for that. His definition is a different one: "*Symmetria est ex ipsius operis membris conveniens consensus ex partibusque ad universae figurae speciem ratae partis responsus*". This rather pompous statement reads in [English] translation, "Symmetry is the concordance of the parts of a structure in relation to the whole figure". Thus, the parts must *concord* with each other and with the overall building; they must *correspond* with each other. Without doubt this *consensus* and *responsus* are to be understood as meaning the similarity of the forms of the parts and of the whole.

Let us consult the ancient master of geometry, Euclid. In Book VI of the *Elements*, where he deals with the similarity of figures, he uses in his definitions and theorems the term "analogous". Thus for example in the 4th theorem, "If triangles have equal angles, the sides opposite equal angles are analogous to each other".

In his translation of the *Timaeus* Cicero gave "*proportion*" for the word, "*analogia*".

Let us return from there to Vitruvius, who tells us (III c.1): "*Aedium compositio constat ex symmetria, cuius rationem architecti diligentissime tenere debent. Ea autem paritur a proportionis, quae graece analogie dicitur. Proportio ex ratae partis membrorum in omni opera totiusque commodulato ex qua ratio efficitur symmetriarum*". This means, "the design of temples depends on symmetry, whose rules architects must observe most diligently. Symmetry is dependent on proportion, which

Greeks call 'analogia'. Proportion is the concordance between the diffence parts and of them
with the whole, on which the law of symmetry
depends".

A specific type must be assumed, whose
mass (*modulus*), pattern and prototype are valid
for the whole. The concordance achieved in this
way is what Vitruvius calls "*commodulatio*" (a
literal translation of symmetry).

Indeed, the explanation that Vitruvius gives
after the definition quoted above is a different
one, namely that just as in the human body so
too in a building all parts should repeat a basic
form. To express this did not require that
cumbersome circumlocution for symmetry. Did
Vitruvius perhaps give the Greek definition
without completely understanding it? He
concludes the chapter with the words, "We
marvel at those who, building temples to the
immortal gods, so ordered the parts of their
work that, whether taken separately or as a
whole, their parts were composed so that they
meet the requirements of proportion and
symmetry.

Who these Ancients were who established
these norms of temple architecture, he does not
tell us. But that it originates in the transmission
of a sacred old precepts is certain.

CHAPTER FOUR: PROPORTION
IN EARLY CHRISTIAN AND
MEDIEVAL ARCHITECTURE

Let us attempt to follow this principle
further in the history of architecture. Paganism
vanished; the temples of the gods crumbled;
new ones were no longer built. With the victory
of Christianity the religious tradition of
paganism was broken and extinguished; and
with that too the architectural traditions were
forgotten. Instead of antique temples, Christian
basilicas were built, and church architecture
underwent its own evolution in the buildings of
Ravenna, in the domes buildigns of the
Byzantine Empire, and in the Romanesque and
Gothic architecture of the West.

If the theory of proportion is not merely
arbitrary but rooted, as it seems to us, in the
nature of the thing, in the essence of man, and
in the laws of beauty, then we can expect to find
it to be applied in this new field, too.

No value was attached to the exterior of the
basilica and so we cannot expect any systemic
arrangement here.   The main emphasis was
placed on the appearance of the interior.   The
rule is that the side aisles must have the same
ratio of height to breadth as the center aisle (*San
Apollinaire in classe* in Ravenna, and the cathedral
of Parenzo *fig.* 55). The outstanding effect of the
basilica derives from the long rows of columns
that are of the same size. These show, in

perspective forshortening of progressively diminishing figures, the distance between which also diminishes. It is mainly this feature that gives the uniform rows of columns their beauty.

Early Christian Centralized Buildings

The arrangement of centralized structures is quite different. Already in Roman architecture we find abutments of the dome developing into a circle of niches. These now formed themselves in a manner analogous to the main space. One can observe how, in San Vitale in Ravenna (*fig.* 56), the columns of the niches enclose figures that are similar to those enclosed by the great octagonal piers of the dome. The same is the case with the niches under the great semi-domes of the Sophia church in Constantinople. On the second storey the number of columns on the straight side increased so that the ratio of columnar height to intercolumniation remains the same. There are seven intercolumniations on the upper floor to five on the lower, while the ratio of the storeys' heights is 5 : 7.

It is hardly necessary to refer to the usual plan of the Byzantine church, whose main dome is accompanied by several similar adjoining domes.

Romanesque Churches

In Romanesque churches the concordance between the central and side aisles, and main and lateral apses, is only approximate. The round-arched frieze and the low-arched gallery play a similar role, by repeating the row of arches beneath them, as the triglyph frieze does above the row of columns. The proportions of the stories is often determines by the divisions of the openings, so that, for example, where two arched openings stand above an arcade, the upper supports (*Stützen*) are half the height of the lower ones. (Pisa cathedral, Autun cathedral, *Saint Saturnin* in Toulose in *fig.* 57). In the façade, the similarity of the side aisles to the middle aisle is often expressed. In San Zeno in Verona the structure of the portal also repeats the same form.

Gothic Churches

We enter the realm of the Gothic style. It is the furthest removed from classical, and breaks completely with the antique traditions. It remains associated, to some extent, with older church architecture, but for the rest it evolves a very distinctive character. This consists of having all large forms replicated in details or echoed in smaller parts. Pinnacles, gablets and blind tracery are repetitions of spires, gables and window tracery. The way in which these elements grow out of the body of the building corresponds with the growth of a tree which, in its branching out, even in its tenderest shoots, always recalls a specific original form. Where these subsidiary details do not overwhelm the structure one discovers examples of simple and clear concordance/ Thus in the Elizabeth church in Marburg. Here the figure of the entire tower is repeated in the four smaller towers, and is repeated again in the tall panel of the main storey with its narrow window.

The loveliest window traceries develop from stronger and weaker mullions, so that the smaller divisions repeat the larger, and the lesser imitates the whole. With concordance in the main outline, the greatest variety is required in the remaining pieces in order to avoid monotony and to produce a pleasant contrast.

The capitals of the shafts of a Gothic pier are often decorated with leaves, whose ribs or stems bend over, emerge out of or cross over each other, just like the ribs of the vaults above them. Here too the small is a prelude to what will appear on a large scale.

We limit ourselves here to not that the facades with two towers of the most beautiful cathedrals are partitioned to create rectangles that are similar to one another, and that usually the central field with the rose window echoes the entire façade, and that the height of the towers' storeys either continually increase as they climb higher, to create an impression of upward striving, or else diminish in the same proportion as the stories become narrower as we see in the minarets of Cairo, whose beauty arises from the similarity in the proportions of their stories and at the same time in the variations of their decoration.

The examples presented here suffice to show that the Gothic made extensive and free use of the principle of the repetition of the large in the small.

Proportions in Renaissance and Modern Architecture: Churches in the Italian Renaissance

The Middle Ages drew to a close; chivalry and romantic poetry withered away. The great Gothic cathedrals remained unfinished. One of the great shifts in taste got under way. People searched for other ideals and fixed their gaze on classical antiquity which were scarcely known or heeded. It was out of admiration for it that the architecture of the Renaissance sprang.

Also brought back to life and to a new esteem was the fundamental principle of architectural proportion.

Whether architects first adopted it in practice and then theorized about it, or the other way round; indeed, whether with or without clear awareness, is unclear. But that they adopted it is certain, for it shines out from the most beautiful monuments of the Italian Renaissance. The same beautiful proportions as in Antiquity emerge again, and concordance is no longer approximate but appears with strong geometric precision. In its rich development the architecture of the Renaissance offers an even greater abundance of examples and proofs than the relics of Antiquity. The examples present themselves at every step that one takes with a guide like that of Bühlmann in hand.[10]

In church architecture, Brunelleschi employed the same ratio of breadth to height for the central and side aisles (San Lorenzo and Santo Spirito in Florence); Baccio Pintelli brought the same concordance to church facades in Rome. In churches with single aisles, of which the model was provided by Alberti in Sant' Andrea, Mantua, the apses between the abutments repeat the figure of the transept, and are in the same relation to them as the smaller niches are to the apses themselves. This can be seen all the more decidedly in the church of Santa Maria de Monti in Rome.[11]

The division of Roman triumphal arches (the outline of the side passages analogous to the central one), appears again in the tomb of the

---

[10] *Die Architektur des classischen Alterthums und der Renaissance.* Stuttgart 1872-77.

[11] See Burckhardt, J, *Geschichte der Renaissance in Italian.* Stuttgart 1868, p.135.

doge Vendramin in Venice, as well as one those of the prelates in Santa Maria del Populo in Rome. This subordination of the side arches to the main arch is at its simplest in the cross-section of the church of St Salvatore in Venice, which is repeated in the altars and wall tombs of the church.[12]

In centralized churches smaller domes follow the main dome in plan and elevation (comp. Bramante's plan for St Peter's in Rome (*fig.* 58). Moreover, the tambour beneath the dome became an upper storey and on the outside had the same relationship of breadth to height as the entire structure of the church below it. Examples are S. Pietro in Montorio at Rome (*fig.* 59), Bramante's Consolazione in Todi, and the structure of St Peter's as planned by Michaelangelo (*fig.* 60). It is not the least of Michaelangelo's merits that when he built St Peter's he succeeded in preserving this concordance by furnishing the exterior of the church with a single great order of pilasters and repeated in its relationship to the attic the order of the columns of the tambour. (Comp. the analogous in the structure of the upper and lowerer storeys of the Roman triumphal arch in *fig.* 43).

---

[12] Burckhardt, *op.cit.,* p.143.

Private Buildings of the Italian Renaissance

Turning to private buildings, which appear in a variety of forms, we find the same law in all their parts, whether large or small.

The proportions of every part of the main structure, whether original or appended to it, must be in concordance with each other. The upper storey of the Pitti palace in Florence mirrors the entire structure (it is half as long and half as tall); the projecting porticoes of the Villa Rotonda (*fig.* 61) repeat the form of the building, etc.

Components of the Façade

The rule for the components of the façade was first formulated in Florence: what the string course is to a single storey, the entablature is to the entire palace. This rule was first applied, and with great success, to the Strozzi palace (*fig.* 62).

The total height is divided into three equal parts. Each of the two lower storeys terminates in a string course which, with the course of blocks below it, makes up one-eighth of the storey's height. Crowning all three storeys, the entablature is three times the height of a string course and with its frieze is one-eighth the height of the overall structure.

The same is the case with the Piccolomini palace in Siena. On the Gondi palace in

Florence, the lower storey is marked off as a lower structure by stronger rustication, and the entablature is brought into proportion with the two upper storeys alone in that it is double the height of the string course.

This is also the disposition of most palaces in Rome. The string course that crowns they lower storey and demarcates it as substructure, has the same proportion to it as the entablature does to the other parts of the façade (in the Negroni palace in the ratio of 1 : 12). These facades however lack the simplicity and decisiveness shown by those in Florence. The Farnese palace is more effective because it follows the simple division of the Strozzi palace and ends up in an entablature and frieze that is in relationship to the whole as as the string courses and their friezes are to the individual storeys. The entablature here again is three times the height of the string course is one does not compare their perpendicular heights instead of the actual distance between the upper and lower edges, whose dimensions would at least be foreshortened by perspective.

Window and Door Frames

There are rules for the frames (architraves) of windows and doors that lead back to Antiquity. When a window opening is markedly higher than wide, enclosing it with a frame of the same width is somewhat unsatisfactory. This stupidity (*Ungereimtheit*) is more evident with wide frames or with narrow windows than with narrow frames or broad windows. The frames of tall windows need to be augmented above or below, or both above and below, so that the outer and inner outline the same. For openings that are horizontal, on the other hand, the frame on the sides can be strengthened (*fig.* 63). The windows and portals of the Renaissance thus resemble the cella of an ancient temple, which was enclosed by columns and their entablatures that made its exterior and interior outlines the same.

When a simple window frame directly abuts a string course, it takes on the treatment of the enclosure and as a result the interior and exterior outlines are identical (window of Massimi palace in Rome).

Usually, the breadth and height of the border is determined simply by the diagonal of the opening. This is the case when pilasters or half-columns are added to frames of uniform width, as in the Farnese, Bartolini, Pandolfini, etc., palaces (*figs.* 64, 65) following the prototype of the aedicula of the Pantheon.

With these examples, one recalls that a part of the window aperture is covered by the parapet (comp. also the examples of Bühlmann's *Architektur des classischen Alterthums und der Renaissance.* Part II, Stuttgart 1875, plate 41).

Peruzzi and Vignola used these diagonals mostly for the frames of doorways, even though a base like that was impractical there.

For example, if the width of the door frame is one-third that of the height, the lintel with its cap must be one-third the clear height of the doorway (*figs.* 71, 72). Or if the opening of the doorway is twice as high as wide, the lintel is twice the width of the frame.

Wall Openings and Surfaces

Of particular importance is the relationship of a wall opening to the wall surfaces that surround it.

Florence again offers outstanding examples.

The proportions are most clearly evidence if one expands an arched window opening into a rectangle and draws its diagonals. This results either in the diagonals of two adjoining windows intersecting under a line delineating the upper border of the wall surface (*fig.* 67); or in the elongated diagonals intersecting a lower and an upper opening (*fig.* 68). In the first case, the wall surface is divided by the axes of the piers in such a way that it serves the window opening as a proportionately equal enclosure; in the second case, the entire wall surrounds the opening with proportionately equal space.

The first way is found in the Pitti palace in Florence (*fig.* 69) and in more or less exactly the same way in most Roman palaces, with dominant wall surfaces, particularly the Bartolini and Pandolfine palaces in Florence (*figs.* 64 and 65).The second type of concordance is employed in the Riccardi, Strozzi, Gondi and Guadagni palaces. With the width of the pier equaling the width of the window, the height of the wall above is equal to the height of the window (upper storey of the Strozzi palace in *fig.* 70). With the piers narrower than the openings, as in the Guadagni palace (*fig.* 71), the height of the wall above the apex of the arch is in the same proportion lower as the windows.[13] In this example the first type of concordance is also achieved.

The observation that the smooth wall surfaces between and above the windows must be of the same width refers back to the first type of concordance and is valid on condition that the height of the window is twice its width (Pitti, Bartolini, Pandolfini palaces).

Ordering of Pilasters and Columns

The same requirements pertain to the arrangement of orders of pilasters on a façade. The base of the pillar is intimately related to the base of the window beside it. They either form

---

[13] [*sic*: "…so sind auch dir Mauerhöhen über den Bogen- scheiten in dem selben Verhältnis niedriger, als die Fenster".]

figures that resemble each other or the order of pilasters flanks the sides of the window and above it along its diagonals and at proportionately equal distances, thereby participating in the enclosure. Examples of the first type are the lower storey of the Farnesina (*fig.* 72), the Stoppani and Uguccioni palaces by Raphael, and also the Porto palace in Vicenza. Examples of the other type are upper storeys of the Farnesina, the courtyard façade of the Massimi palace and the main floor of the Ossoli palace, all by Peruzzi. The concordance – in the sense of geometric similarity - of the window and pilaster bases is achieved by Michaelangelo (the Senate), Galeazzo Alessi, Sansovino and Palladio where, as far as possible, the rule is obeyed that the pairs of supports should be made as different as is feasible. Fashioned window frames are juxtaposed with plain pilasters; these contrast again with half-columns, herms or rusticated columns.

The early Renaissance in Venice, too, has beautiful examples (Scuola di San Marco).

The same relationships also determine the way in which pilasters and columns are combined with arcades. Pairs of pillars or pilasters enclose a pair of piers, as they do with the Theater of Marcellus and with the Roman triumphal arches (arcades by Peruzzi, Palladio – *fig.* 37 – etc.). Palladio's basilica in Vicenza owes its harmonious appearance to this concordance, notwithstanding the awkward way it spreads out (*fig.* 74); the base of the small columns is treated in a way analogous to pedestals of the large order.

Division of Wall Surfaces

The division of wall surfaces likewise observance of the law that the parts of a figure must correspond to the whole. This holds true above all of the main field of the surface that stands out by virtue of its size or decoration. One frequently notices this concordance on wall paintings in Pompeii; it is continued in the Renaissance and is generally employed in the Rococo. Examples are found in the main room of the Massimi palace (*fig.*75), in the rooms of the Caprarola palace and in the assembly chamber of the Grand Council of the Doge's palace in Venice. It is very common to find that the door of a room is placed near the corner, and takes away relatively as much from the wall's length as the dado does from its height.

The same holds true of facades, if the windows cluster together of if their occur segments of different widths.

In Padua's Del Consiglio palace,[14] the central group of windows of the upper storey is

---

[14] See Bühlmann, J. *Die Architektur des classischen Alterthums und der Renaissance.* Part 2. Stuttgart 1875. Plate 47/

similar to the main portion and to the entire façade and that of the loggia of the Sapienza in Naples to the whole. Prominent figures in the partitions of the doors correspond with the entire door, and are surrounded by moldings that mirror the moldings of the doorways (doors of the Vatican, etc.). Thus in particular during the Rococo period.

Structure of Details

The structure of details, too, is subject to the law of analogy. Window enclosures with pediments form a structure analogous to houses. The window entablature corresponds to the main entablature; its projection and height are determined by it. The number of times that the entablature goes into the height of the façade is the number of times that the entablature of the window goes into the height of the window frame (see *fig.* 65). The cornice and frieze of the Pandolfini palace go eight times into its overall height, and the window entablature, which corresponds with all parts of the main entablature, goes eight times into the height of the aedicula. In the Bartolini palace (see *fig.* 64) the corresponding ratios are 1 : 8 and 1 : 7. Where the ground floor is a substructure, the entablature corresponds to the remaining height of the façade. This is only approximately so in the many-storied palaces of Rome.

If for example the height of the window frame is one-third that of the façade, its entablature must only be one-third of the main cornice (Sciarra and Negroni palaces in Rome). The entablatures of facades that have orders of pilasters or columns determine the window lintels, if these do not simultaneously function as the main entablature (comp. *fig.* 72).

Profiles and Ornamentation

Profiles too bespeak an effort to make the smaller parts accord with the large. The cornice that they support and the segments that lie in their shade, as well as the frieze beneath them, form a group that is repeated in the profile of the architrave (in its upper part or in the whole). Peruzzi and Vignola have a preference for this type of division and arrange the parts of the architrave in a progressively diminishing series (*fig.* 76).

Antiquity's concordance between the profile of capital and entablature was employed again. The height and projection of the abacus are proportional to one another, and the necking of the pilaster's capital is analogous to that of the frieze's ornament. Rosettes on the necking of the column correspond to the intermittent (*intermittierenden*) decoration of the triglyph frieze, and the foliage on the capital to a foliated frieze. Beautiful examples are provided by the early Venetian Renaissance and the orders of Alberti, Bramante, etc.[15]

This law extends to the divisions of ornaments. The acanthus leaf is divided into individual parts and these into similarly-formed lobes. Arabian ornamentation repeats the continuous principal form in delicate interwoven elements.

The German Renaissance

It would be superfluous to trace this principle in all other architectural styles. The German Renaissance is marked more by a rich combination of different forms than by beautiful proportions. We will point out here only that on the much-admired façade of the Otto-Heinrich building in the Heidelberg castle (*fig.* 77), with its diversity of forms, there is a strong concordance in the relationship of the double windows and the order of pilasters.

The Statements of Alberti

Turning again to the Renaissance, the question presents itself again of whether the builders of that time, who obeyed the law so faithfully, also articulated it as theory. What

---

[15] Comp. Bühlmann, J. *Die Architektur des classischen Alterthums und der Renaissance.* Stuttgart 1872-77.

Vitruvius was as an authority in Antiquity, Leon Battista Alberti of Florence (d. 1472) was for the 15th century. This architect, who at the sametime was also the founder of Renaissance theory, enunciated the leading idea in another – though intelligible – version.

At the outset of his work *De Re Aedificatoria* there is a chapter on *lineamenta,* which calls for the angles and lines of parts of a structure to correspond to one another in specific directions and specific connections (*adnotando et praefiniendo angulos et lineas certa directione et certa connexione*). Book VI (cap. 5) presents a description of a good design that concludes with: "*Omnia ad certos angulos paribus lineis adaequanda*".[16] (Comp. further the passages quoted by J. Burckhardt[17] VI, cap. 2; IX, cap. 3 and 5.)

Previously-drawn lines and angles are thus a tool for attaining proportional figures.

It was in this way that architects achieved that "rhythm of mass" ("*Rhythmus des Massen*") which, according to the greatest scholar of the Renaissance, J. Burckhardt, was what gave the architecture of the Cinquecento its artistic quality.

Shifting our focus to the masterpieces of modern architecture, we find that they too

---

[16] [trans: "Everything must be adjusted to fixed angles by parallel lines".]

[17] *Geschichte der Renaissance in Italien.* Stuttgart 1868, p.41.

provide confirmation of what we found in the Ancients and followed through the Middle Ages. We cite only the facades of the main Guard House and the Museum in Berlin by Shinkel (*fig.* 79), the Old Pinakothek and Propyleum in Munich by Klenze (*fig.* 78), and leave to the reader the analysis of these buildings. In the last-mentioned example two concordances to be distinguished from one another. The upper stories of the towers are analogous to the entrance hall, as are the doors are to the whole towers.

The rule is so obvious, and is applied so widely, that in uncountable numbers of domestic houses today facades are partitioned according to similarity of figures. A group of windows or a richly-articulated portion of the façade repeat the main figure; or the form of a window corresponds to the section of the façade to which it belongs, etc.

It is moreover a correct instinct that in the frames of copperplate engravings and similar objects the margins of the narrow side are wider than those on the long side, or that in the decoration of titlepages the design encloses a form that corresponds to the entire page.

CHAPTER FIVE: FINAL OBSERV-
ATIONS.
Proportion and Variety.

There is an undeniable need to ask what the basis is of a law that is applicable to such a variety of phenomena. Let us try to deepen our understanding of it.

A distinguished aesthetician has declared, "Sculpture is an imitation of humans, architecture the imitation of plants". Inorganic nature provides geometric elements, organic nature provides in plants, and especially in the growth of trees, the prototype of construction, the repetition of the basic form in the individual parts: or in other words, the law of similarity and proportion. The whole form of a tree is reflected in the branch; it often even appears in the form of leaves and fruit.

In the plant world this repetition arises from growth, at the beginning the delicate twigs strengthen into branches and the embryo a complete organism. The whole grows out of a basic form and develops itself into numerous variations.

There is however yet another reason for the pleasurable effect, and this is based on the ability of the mind to compile from images seen from various perspectives an idea of the whole. The simpler the relation of the parts to each other, and the more frequently these repeat themselves, the more easily and willingly does the eye follow the lines, and the more satisfyingly does it construct the overall image.

Mere similarity of figures without variation and contrast would, with justification, be considered monotonous and boring. For just this reason, this law requires contrast to complete it, just as contrast requires proportion for its completion. Contrast without some common elements becomes annoying, merely, or irritating, or ridiculous.

Harmony

The aesthetic judgement of the eye is gratified by variety that contains analogous forms. Does that not hold true, too, of the aesthetic judgement of the ear? What else is rhyme, from which the distinctive magic of modern poetry derives, other than a similarity of sounds that are never identical, and and that captivate us precisely by their interweaving of variety and change? We now recognize rhythm in architecture, too.

Similar rules are found in music. The world of sounds and the world forms indicate beauty with the same concept and term: harmony.

Harmony in architecture is precisely the analogy of the parts to the whole: *partium et totius operis commodulatio*, as old Vitruvius said.

No rule in art can can make up for a lack of genius. The diligent use of a rhyming dictionary does not make someone a poet; yet a poet must be careful to obey the rules of rhythm.

By the same token, a knowledge of the law presented here will never make someone an architect. But it will serve someone with talent by minimizing the need for experimentation and by avoiding excesses. It directs him to the healthy limits within which genius must operate in order to produce work that gratifies aesthetic feeling and at the same time can justify itself to the inquiring mind.

The End

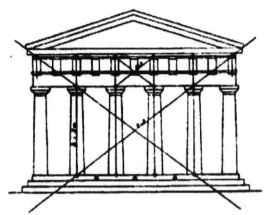

Fig. 1 Ratios of the archaic Doric style

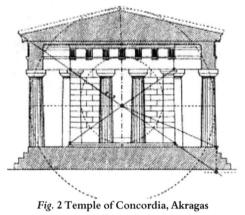

Fig. 2 Temple of Concordia, Akragas

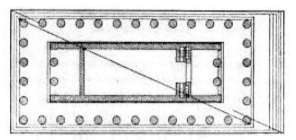

Fig. 3 Temple of Juno Lacinia in Akragas

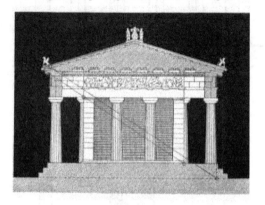

Fig. 4 Temple of Athena at Aegina

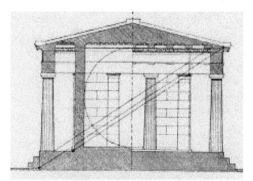

Fig. 5 Temple of Nemesis at Rhamnus

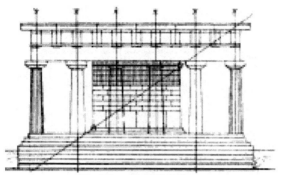

Fig. 6 Temple "D", Selinus

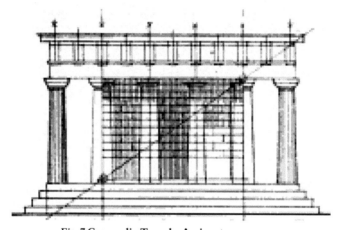

Fig. 7 Concordia Temple, Agrigentum

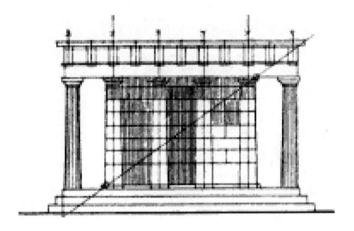

Fig. 8 Temple of Nemesis, Rhamnus

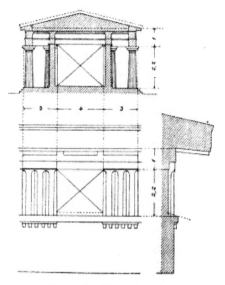

Fig. 9 Temple of Poseidon, Paestum

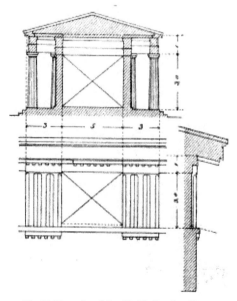

Fig. 10 Temple of Apollo Epikurios, Bassae

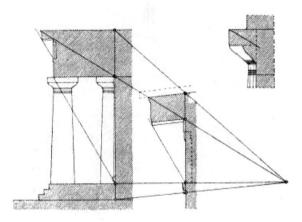

Fig. 11 Temple of Poseidon, Paestum

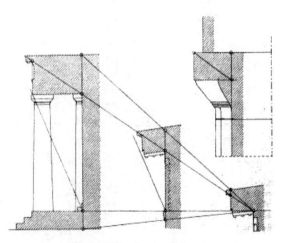

Fig. 12 Parthenon, Athens

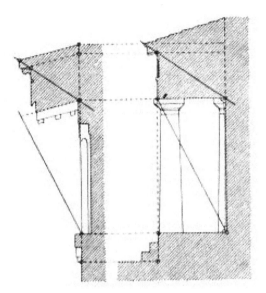

Fig 13 Temple of Aegina, Athens

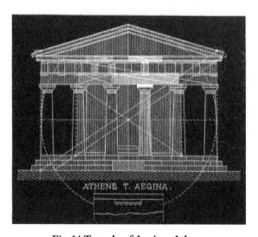

Fig. 14 Temple of Aegina, Athens

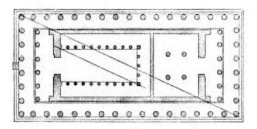

Fig. 15 The Parthenon, Athens

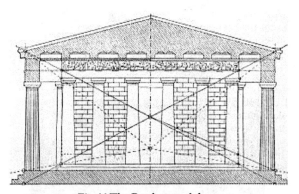

Fig. 16 The Parthenon, Athens

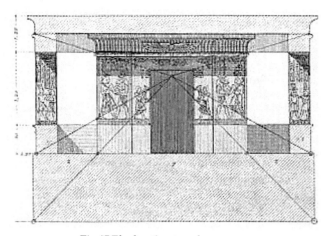

Fig. 17 Elephantine temple

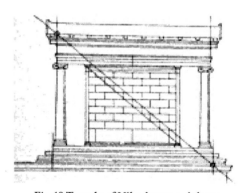

Fig. 18 Temple of Nike Apteros, Athens

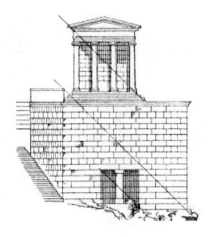

Fig. 19 Temple of Nike Apteros, Athens

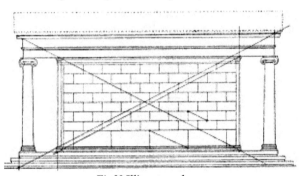

*Fig.*20 Illisus temple

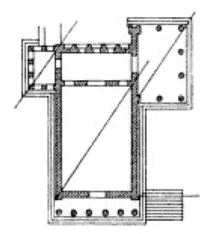

Fig. 21 Erechtheion, Athens

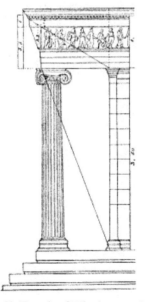

*Fig.*22 Temple of Nike Apteros, Athens

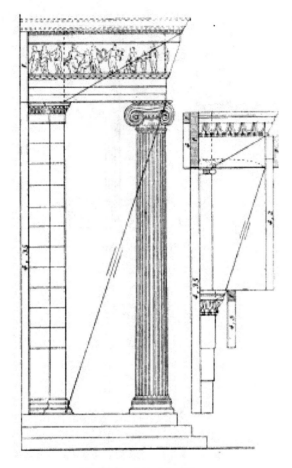

Fig. 23 Erechtheion, Athens

Fig. 24 Erechtheion, Athens

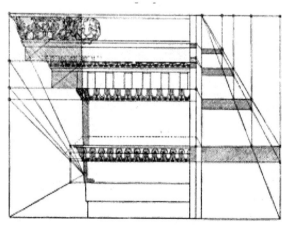

Fig. 25 From the Temple of Athena Polias, Priene

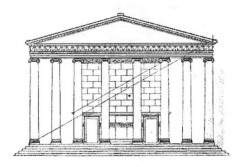

Fig. 26 Temple of Zeus, Aizanoi

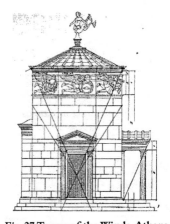

Fig. 27 Tower of the Winds, Athens

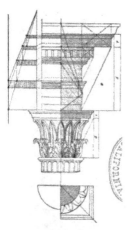

Fig. 28 Tower of the Winds, Athens

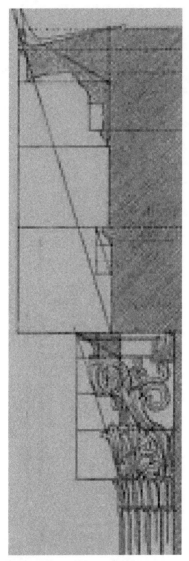

Fig. 29 Choragic Monument of Lysicrates, Athens

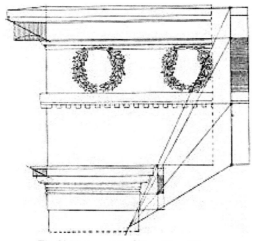

Fig. 30 Monument of Trasyllus, Athens

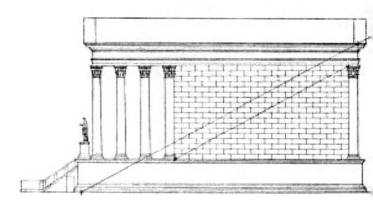

Fig. 31 Temple of Antoninus and Faustina, Rome

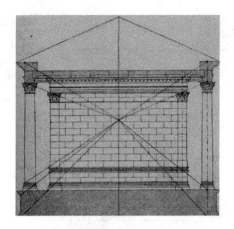

Fig. 32 Temple of Jupiter, Baalbek

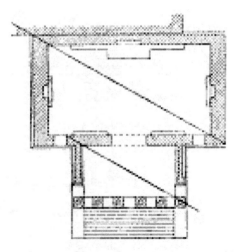

Fig. 33 Temple of Concordia, Rome

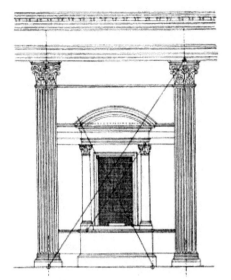

Fig. 34 Pantheon, Rome

Fig. 35 Gate of the river at Chamas

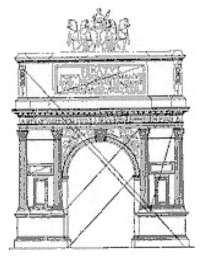

Fig 38 Arch of Titus, Rome

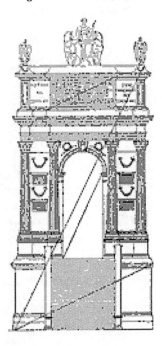

Fig. 37 Triumphal gate of Hadrian, Ancona

Fig. 39 Gate of Hadrian, Athens

Fig. 40 Triumphal arch of Septimius Severus, Rome

Fig. 41 Triumphal arch of Constantine, Rome

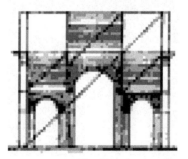

Fig. 42

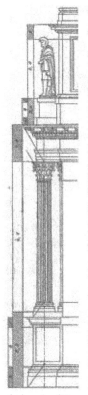

Fig. 43 Triumphal arch of Constantine, Rome

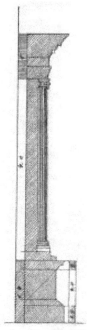

Fig. 44 Temple of Fortuna Virilis, Rome

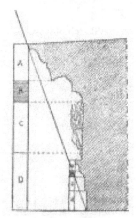

Fig. 45 Temple of Vesta, Tivoli

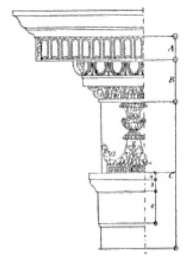

Fig. 46 Temple of Antoninus and Faustina, Rome

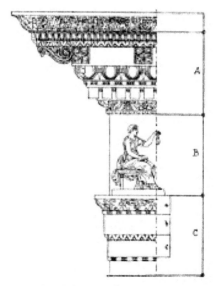

Fig. 47 Forum of Nerva, Rome

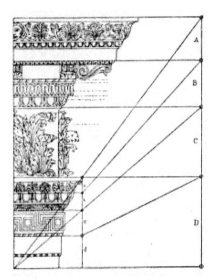

Fig. 48 Temple of Jupiter, Palmyra

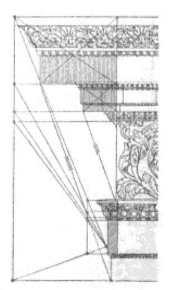

Fig. 49 Frontispiece of Nero, Rome

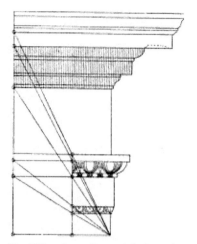

Fig. 50 Pantheon, Rome (*afer Desgodes*)

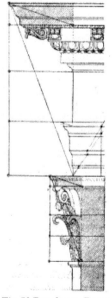

Fig. 50 Pantheon, Rome

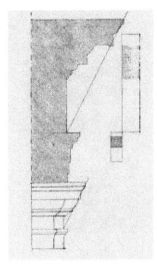

Fig. 52 Colosseum, Rome

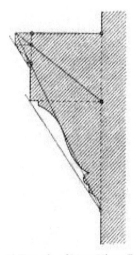

Fig. 53 Temple of Mars Ultor, Rome

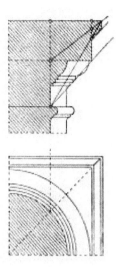

Fig. 54 Theater of Marcellus, Rome

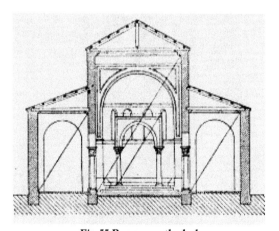

Fig. 55 Parenzo cathedral

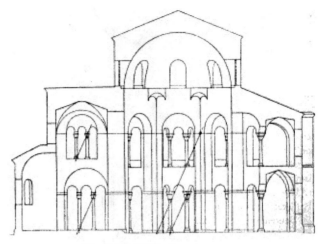

Fig. 56 San Vitale, Ravenna

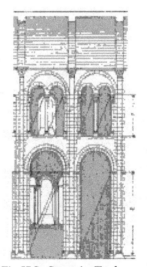

Fig. 57 St. Saturnin, Toulouse

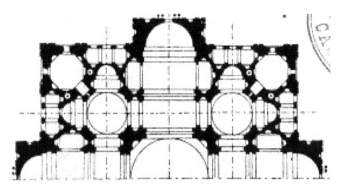

Fig. 58 Bramante's plan for S. Peters, Rome

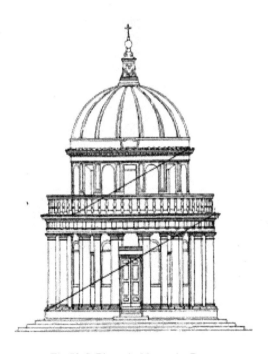

Fig. 59 S. Pietro in Montorio, Rome

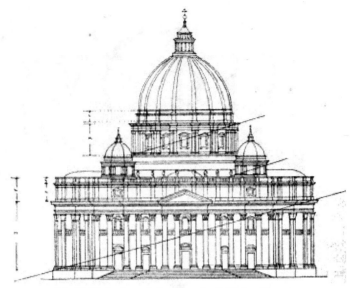

Fig. 60 Michaelangelo's design for S. Pietro, Rome

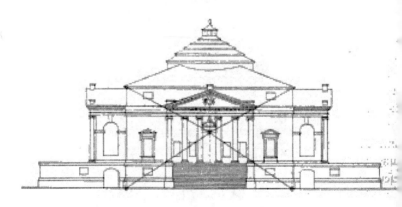

Fig. 61 Villa Rotonda, Vicenza

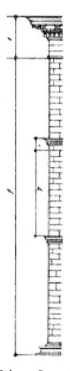

Fig. 62 Palazzo Strozzi, Florence

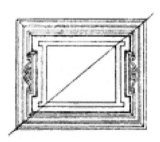

Fig. 63 Palazzo Massimi, Rome

Fig. 64 Palazzo Bartolini, Rome

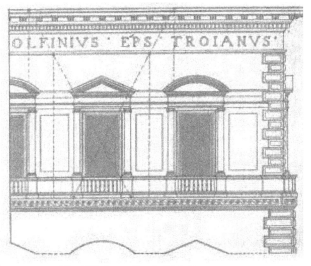

Fig. 65 Palazzo Pandolfini, Rome

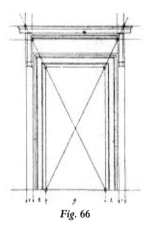

Fig. 66

Figs. 67 (left) and 68 (right)

Fig. 69 Palazzo Pitti, Florence

Fig. 70 Palazzo Strozzi, Florence

Fig. 71 Palazzo Guadagni, Florence

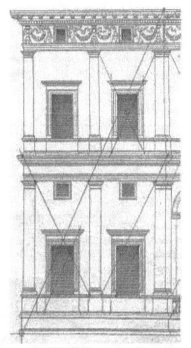

Fig. 72 Villa Farnesina, Rome

Fig. 73 Arcade by Palladio

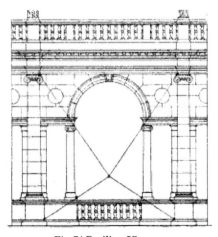

Fig. 74 Basilica, Vicenza

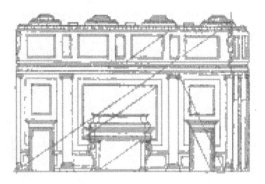

Fig. 75 Interior, Palazzo Massimi, Rome

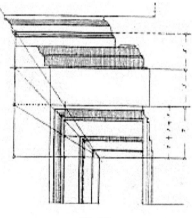

Fig. 76

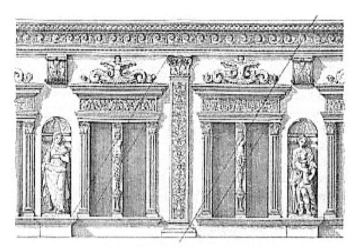

Fig. 77 Interior, Heidelberg Castle

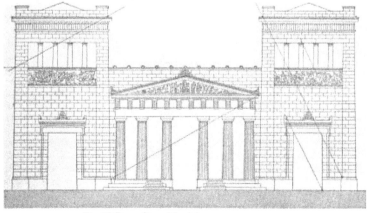

Fig. 78 Propyläen, Munich

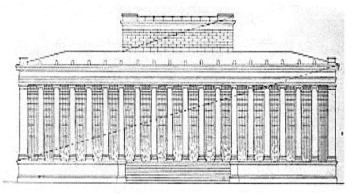

Fig. 79 Museum, Berlin

Heinrich Wölfflin
A Theory of Proportion

Nothing fundamentally new can be added to August Thiersch's brilliant discoveries on the subject of Proportion. Any progress in our knowledge of the character of beautiful proportions can only be an elaboration of Thiersch's Law. What follows here makes no claim beyond that.

"We find by studying the most successful works of all time", says Thiersch, "that in every structure a basic form repeats itself: that the individual parts constitute similar figures in their arrangement and form. Harmony arises from the repetition of the main figure of a work in its subdivisions."

Thiersch's observations present us with an astonishing perspective for he has addressed one half, indeed the greater half, of the problem: there are *consistent proportioons,* not just in the obvious sense that he identifies, but also in the *opposite sense,* in which h:b = B:H.

A few examples will show how meaningful and multifaceted this elaboration of Thiersch's Law can be in practice.

Illustrations 1 and 2 (the Temple of Zeus in Olympia and the Temple of Athena on Aegina). Archaic-Doric style. Determination of proportions for the positioning of the pillars. A middle intercolumniation[18] (reckoned from pillar axis to pillar axis) is inversely proportional to the front rectangle, whose width is determined by the width of the entablature, and whose height reaches from the stylobate to the geison. A diagonal of the front rectangle bisects at right angles the other diagonal of the right angle of the pillars. The Law is validated in quite different situations.[19]

Illustrations 3 and 4 (Erechtheion, east and north sides). High Ionic style. Determination of proportions for the positioning of the pillars. The applicability of the Law is not as apparent as it is in the Archaic Doric style. The more developed art wants to demonstrate the Law only in as it were a concealed manner. The columnar rectangle no longer manifests itself in a simple measurement from the axis of one column to the next, but calculates the distance from one column to the one after the next; and moreover, it is not the axis that is the determining line but the (inner) contour. The composition gains in this way a certain floating quality. It is quite understandable that in the Ionic, where the entablature has no triglyphs, which is to say no further vertical lines, can only

---

[18] The outer intercolumniations are recognizably somewhat narrower.

[19] It is possible, on the basis of this Law, to determine the original height of a temple, even where all that remains is merely the position of the columns.

determine the height of the large (front) rectangle only on the basis of the height of the columnar Order.

Illustration 5 (the façade of Santa Maria Novella in Florence; L. B. Alberti). Thiersch too found that the upper and lower structures are homogenous. What is new is the demonstration that the scheme for the wall incorporates both the upper and the lower diagonals. The corner panels, by contrast, (where it is the same whether one measures from the center of one pilaster to the center of the next, or whether one takes the approach shown in the drawing). The same relationship is repeated below. I shall leave the picture to speak for itself.

Illustration 6 (Cancelleria in Rome, uppermost floor on the wings; Bramante). The two windows and the middle pilaster field are related, in their proportion, to the entire expanse of the pilaster Order.

Illustration 7 (Villa Farnesina in Rome; B. Peruzzi or more probably Raphael). Every wing repeats in reverse the overall expanse of the central structure and of the other wings. In this way it conveys an impression of unshakeable integration ("*Zusammengehörigkeit*") that is so attractive that the relationship of the gently projecting wings is not immediately apparent.

Examples of this kind of proportionality can readily be multiplied: the ones given here will suffice to validate the general principle.

The End

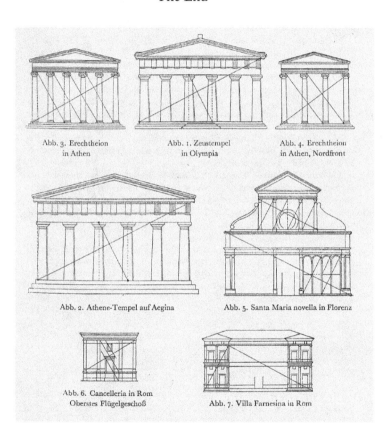

Abb. 3. Erechtheion in Athen

Abb. 1. Zeustempel in Olympia

Abb. 4. Erechtheion in Athen, Nordfront

Abb. 2. Athene-Tempel auf Aegina

Abb. 5. Santa Maria novella in Florenz

Abb. 6. Cancelleria in Rom Oberstes Flügelgeschoß

Abb. 7. Villa Farnesina in Rom

Illustrations 1-7